Cheerleading Secrets

Janey Trishon

SHELFLESS

CHEERLEADING SECRETS
Published by Shelfless Ltd.
Copyright ©2005–2013 Janey Trishon
All rights reserved.

Second Edition (2.2) published 2012, revised 2013

ISBN 978-1490987545

CONTENTS

INTRODUCTION

Cheerleading has been around for a long time. It is something that many girls like to think about starting at a very young age. They imagine standing in a gym cheering for the basketball game, or out on the football field, doing cheers at half time. If you're a parent, at a very early age your children may have already talked you into buying them that first set of play pom-poms. You may have even sat back and watched them perform a cheer or two that they made up just for you.

Young children enjoy making up simple cheers for everything that happens. If you cook their favorite meal they will cheer for a job well done. If you plan a day of fun and amusement they may cheer all the way to your destination. Young children have so much excitement and enthusiasm to spread around. It seems they never get tired.

This is what cheerleading is all about, showing excitement and encouraging others to participate in the fun. Being able to motivate others is a key factor in cheerleading. You need the energy of a child to keep the pace it requires to support and encourage your team. Cheerleaders help to keep the audience excited and lift everyone's spirit.

It takes a special type of person to be a cheerleader. You must be dedicated and loyal. You must be willing to sacrifice personal time to practice and learn cheers. While many of your friends may be meeting to see a movie together, you may be preparing for a game. You must be willing to make these sacrifices to be able to succeed as a cheerleader.

Cheerleaders are always in the spotlight, even when you are not on the sidelines cheering for your team. Classmates and school newspapers always want to know what's going on in your life. You have to be willing to be in the public eye.

You set examples for many other people, especially younger children whose dream is to be a cheerleader one day. They look up to you and follow your examples, good and bad. That is why it is so important to make sure you set good examples in everything you do.

A cheerleader will smile and encourage others even when they are having a problem, or simply just feeling bad. They are the ones who cheer their team on to victory during a difficult game. If their team is defeated, cheerleaders will be there to help them get ready for the next game by building up their confidence. This helps the team to get ready and be motivated for the next game. Cheerleaders are a vital part of any sports team.

Cheerleading is very athletic and requires you to be in good physical condition. It takes a lot of effort to perform many of the cheers and routines. Much of today's cheerleading includes stunts that require coordination, balance and lots of team work.

Cheerleading is one of the best ways to show school spirit and pride. A cheerleader supports all the team activities from football to basketball. They help put enthusiasm and spirit in pep rallies. To be a cheerleader you have to possess leadership qualities.

If you are considering becoming a cheerleader, I hope to answer many of the questions that you may have in this book. I hope to give you a good overview on what cheerleading is all about with as much information as possible.

THE HISTORY OF CHEERLEADING

It seems as though a form of cheerleading has been around for as long as anyone can remember. Cheerleading began many years ago, but the first cheer that was ever recorded in our history was produced in the 1880's. A pep club from Princeton University was motivated to chant and created a cheer for one of their football games.

Cheerleading has been growing every since. Johnny Campbell started the cheerleading as we know it today in 1898. This undergraduate stood up at a football game and yelled "Rah, Rah, Rah..." this is a famous cheer still used today. Because of this act at the University of Minnesota, cheerleading began officially in the year 1898 on November 2nd.

The 1900's brought about a lot of changes for cheerleading. Using the megaphone at games to yell out cheers or chants became very popular. This really helped to lift the spirits of the audience and the players during games. After this around 1920, women started to become very active in cheerleading. The cheerleaders from the University of Minnesota began adding tumbling and gymnastic to their cheers making them even more exciting.

Paper pom-poms were made and used at universities and high schools in the 1930's. During the next ten years the first cheerleading company was formed. This was done by a man who lived in Dallas, Texas named Lawrence R. Herkimer. After this, cheerleaders in colleges started holding meetings and began teaching the basic skills needed to be a cheerleader.

By the 1960's a man named Fred Gastoff invented the vinyl pom-poms. They were introduced to cheerleading by the International Cheerleading Foundation. By the seventies, cheerleading had finally been recognized as an athletic activity. It is an activity that requires both skills and persistence along with hard work and dedication, to accomplish.

Cheerleaders began appearing at all school sports. This is the time when cheerleading camps were formed to train students and coaches. Several colleges began offering credits for cheerleading and a four year letter program, some even offered college scholarships.

The 1980's brought about a lot of changes. One of these changes included cheerleaders becoming involved in community services. On a national level, the media considered the most important group in school to increases spirit and attitude was cheerleading. They became know as leaders in the schools and were well respected for all the effort they put into creating cheers.

Cheerleading has come a long way since that first cheer was introduced. The enthusiasm they help bring out at games makes a huge impact on how well teams play. Cheerleaders continue to cheer on their team in all circumstances good or bad, helping to build the team's confidence.

This is what it is all about, motivating your team to victory. Cheerleaders always try to set good examples and show great leadership within their squad. They are considered role models by many people. They are well disciplined and are highly respected for the efforts they put forth.

Cheerleaders of today spend many hours practicing and training to stay physically fit to be able to perform well for their team. Their goal is to be encouraging and supportive under any circumstances. Most would agree they do their job well.

One thing is for sure - cheerleading has become very popular today. Everyone looks forward to watching the cheerleaders full of spirit and energy cheering their team on to victory. We look forward to seeing them at all the games, everything from junior high school to professional games. Without cheerleaders, sports just wouldn't be same.

Is Cheerleading A Sport?

The question as to whether cheerleading is a sport or not will be answered differently depending on who you talk with. Many cheerleaders feel that because they do all the same things that the players of sports do, then cheerleading should also be a sport. For example, they practice many hours working hard on their cheers and routines. Cheerleaders have to stay physically fit having a good exercise program in place. They may not put in as many hours of practice as a player does, but they do put out a lot of time and effort.

Some schools feel that cheerleading should be considered a sport. In Wake County, North Carolina the schools now officially consider it to be a sport. This was a big step for cheerleading. It opened up the door for many who could not have made a cheerleading squad otherwise. The reason for this is because by making it a sport, you make cheerleading less expensive. Parents won't have to pay for everything which gives a wider variety of students a chance to tryout.

Even though many believe cheerleading should be a sport and some choose to call it as such, nationwide cheerleading is still officially considered an activity in the US.

BECOMING A CHEERLEADER

Becoming a cheerleader is the dream many young girls have. This is a wonderful dream that they can make happen. Becoming a cheerleader has many advantages. For one it is a great way to make friends. It teaches you how to work together as a team to accomplish whatever you set out to do. This is something that will help a child grow and build self confidence, encouraging them to try new things. The character that cheerleading builds is something people can carry with them the rest of their life.

It takes an extraordinary person to become a cheerleader, lots of hard work and dedication. No mater how good or bad you may feel, you still have to provide inspiration for your team whenever it is needed. This is a quality you have to work at and make happen. How many people do you know that could cheer others on with a smile when they really feel like staying in bed? It's not as easy as it may look. Cheerleading requires pushing on to accomplish what is needed regardless of how you feel personally.

In this respect anyone who wishes to become a cheerleader, wants to learn qualities that will certainly help them later in life. If you have a member of your family that is interested in becoming a cheerleader you should encourage and help them to do so any way possible. One important thing to remember about cheerleaders is that anyone can become one, if they are serious about it. Most cheerleading teams can consist of both male and female members.

For those who want to become a cheerleader, but do not have any prior experience, I suggest you start by learning the basic rules and regulations first. It may be that becoming a cheerleader is more involved than you realized. By learning the basic rules you will understand a little of what will be expected of you.

Learning the dos and do nots is essential for making it as a cheerleader. If you break the rules you discredit both your team and the cheerleader image. This is something you cannot afford to let happen. Here are a few simple rules that you would need to follow to be a cheerleader.

Do:

- Stay focused
- Always smile
- Stay alert and energetic
- Be loud enough to be heard
- Always use good manners

Don't:

- Be rude to others
- Let things upset you when cheering
- Have a negative attitude

- Be sluggish

- Give up and not try

Train yourself to have the qualities necessary to be the type of person it takes to be a cheerleader. Let people see you practicing these basic rules in any situation you are involved in. You don't have to wait for an activity, you can show these qualities in a class room. When others see these characteristics in you they will see someone who already possesses many of the qualities needed to be a cheerleader. This is the first step in being recognized for your abilities.

What Becoming A Cheerleader Involves

Now that you know the basic rules, you should take time to learn what being a cheerleader involves. It is a lot more than just jumping around and yelling at games. It involves a large amount of time and dedication to be able to succeed as a cheerleader. It may be more time consuming than you realized at first. Make sure that you will have the time available that becoming a cheerleader will require.

One important thing for you to understand is that cheerleading is very physical. Being able to make it through a game requires a lot of energy. You can only imagine what it will take to last through a season. It is necessary to be physically fit to become a cheerleader. This is the only way you will be able to perform many of the cheers and stunts you will be required to do. A good exercise program combined with a balanced diet is essential. You should have this already in progress before trying out for cheerleading.

There are many things you need to be knowledgeable about. For example, do you know the difference between a cheer and a chant? Do you know the different positions that cheerleaders can have? If you do know what these positions are, do you know what is required to hold each of them? There is a lot of information you should acquire before trying to become a cheerleader. Although it can be a lot of fun and games, it is a lot of hard work as well.

You should take time to learn about the different jumps and how to perform some of them. Learning a few simple cheers and routines wouldn't hurt either. Practice cheering on your own, by doing this you will start out ahead of the game. You can always ask a friend or family member to practice with you so it will be more fun. It would make a good impression on your part if you learned different moves and made up a cheer of your own, before trying out for cheerleader.

The next important thing is to make sure you meet all the other requirements that are involved. Are you wondering what other requirements I could possibly be talking about? Actually there are many things that need to be considered. For starters, your grade level is a very important factor in becoming a cheerleader. If you do not maintain a certain grade level the school will not allow you to participate. Be sure and keep those grades up!

Remember you also have to have your parent's permission to become a cheerleader when you are still in school. This protects the school in case you were to get hurt in practice or at a game. Without your parent's signature showing agreement, you will not be allowed to participate.

Keep in mind the total amount of time that is going to be required once you make a cheerleading squad. Make sure you will have all the extra time needed to put into cheerleading, without burning yourself out. You have to be a hundred percent devoted to cheerleading to be successful.

So you have taken all of the above information and decided this is something you want to do - where do you go from here? What will be your next move? Once you reach this point you are ready for tryouts. You can apply what you have learned so far to help you make the team.

Find out as much information as you can about the tryouts before you sign up. Most tryouts usually last for around two weeks. You will need to attend a meeting that will take place just before the tryouts begin. At this meeting you will be told what will be expected of you and the general rules that apply to the tryouts.

While at the meeting you may be taught some basic jumps and cheers. Theses are ones the judges would like to see you perform at the tryouts. You can practice these at home before having to perform them at the tryout, giving you a little edge. These cheers will show how fast you catch on to new things you are introduced to. This meeting will also give you the chance to ask any questions or voice any concerns you may have.

When the tryouts first begin you may be competing against a lot of others that are very talented, but don't be intimidated by this. You have just as good a chance of making the team as anyone else does, especially if you have been preparing for it.

Everyone will get a chance to show what they have, and the judges will narrow things down by selecting the semi-finalist. At this point the semi-finalist will compete to try and become one of the finalists. From the finalist the winners will be chosen. If it is a small school and not many students attend, tryouts may not last as long or go through as many steps.

Most of all it is important to relax and show self-confidence at all times. The judges are not looking for what you already know, but more for what you will be able to learn. If you show you have the basic skills required for cheerleading you will be one of their first choices.

PARENTAL CONCERNS

All parents know the importance of their children taking part in activities at school. Everyone is proud when their child announces they are interested in an activity or sport. Activities help children learn discipline and how to become a team player. It is an opportunity for them to belong to a group and make new friends.

Activities help children to focus on positive things and avoid the negative. They gives them a good way to spend their time eliminating boredom. Sports and activities give children many advantages they would not have access to otherwise. Even with these advantages, there are still many concerns that parents face.

Safety

One main concern all parents share is keeping their children safe. This is true with any sport or activity including cheerleading. Parents know that a child could be hurt while performing a cheer or routine. After all cheerleading is very athletic and accidents can happen. It would be possible to twist an ankle when doing a cheer or pull a muscle while doing a split or some other move.

Although injuries that are caused from cheerleading are fairly rare, they do occur. It is possible to injure your neck, back or ankles while learning to do moves correctly. The leading injuries that cheerleaders suffer with are those involving the ankles and knees.

This is why safety is a big concern for parents. With all the gymnastics done in cheerleading plus stunts like pyramids, cheerleaders can be injured. The injury rate increases as more difficult stunts are added to the routines.

When the proper safety rules are followed and safety equipment is used, the risk of injuries greatly decreases. Cheerleaders should always practice on mats and wear suitable clothing, including the correct shoes. There should always be a qualified supervisor present during practice sessions and at all games.

The proper training is essential before trying to perform a stunt. This is where many injuries occur. A child tries to learn something new without receiving all the training they need. Never get impatient, if you have not done a move before, make sure you let someone who is qualified teach you how. Trying to learn something on your own could cause you to be injured.

A cheerleader's general health also plays a big part in preventing injuries. The healthier a child is the more they can be alert and focused. This helps them to concentrate and be more careful when performing stunts. By making sure that children eat a well-balance diet, parents can help them stay healthier and safer.

As with any other activity the best way to address safety concerns for cheerleaders is by getting involved. The more you know about your child's activities, the better you will feel. You can talk with the school and your child's coach to make sure proper guidelines are being followed.

Making sure the school has the proper equipment necessary for the activity taking place is a good idea. If for some reason they do not, find out why. If funds are the reason, perhaps you can help find a way to help raise money to buy the right equipment.

Safety also has a lot to do with how well the students are being supervised. Make sure those in charge are qualified to do the job at hand. This is especially true while cheerleaders are practicing and learning new moves. You won't worry as much when you know proper procedures are being followed to ensure your child's safety.

Skimpy Uniforms

As cheerleading has become more and more popular, the uniforms seem to become smaller. Yes its true, skimpy uniforms are a big issue for parents these days. Many parents believe that the majority of the uniforms being worn by cheerleaders are inappropriate.

You can't help but wonder if this is setting a bad example for teenagers. By allowing cheerleaders to wear these skimpy uniforms are we teaching them that this type of dress is okay? Is it encouraging them to dress inappropriate at other events? Is it making activities too sexual? This is a concern that has been around for a while and it looks like one that may be here for a long time to come.

This is a difficult concern to address because so much depends on the personal opinion of each individual. What some people may feel is unacceptable, others feel is perfect. This is what makes the subject so controversial. It is also the reason you have to deal with this concern on a personal level.

The best way to address this issue is for the parents to find out what types of uniforms their child will be wearing. It will then be the parent's decision as to how they feel about the uniforms. You will have an opportunity ahead of time to decide if the uniforms are too skimpy, and if you will allow your child to wear them.

If you do allow your child to wear the uniforms the school has provided, but are not happy with it, you can be a part of choosing the next uniforms. You do this by being involved in school functions like PTA meetings. These types of functions will give you the opportunity to be a part of the decisions made on the uniforms and equipment used by the school.

Being involved is the key to being aware of what is going on in your child's life. Not only will it help relieve many of your concerns, but you can enjoy being a part of something your child is interested in.

Provocative Dance

Just as with the uniforms, dance is also a big issue. Some of the dance steps can appear to be quite provocative to many people, while to others they are not. This is why it is so hard to say what is acceptable in dance moves. What others accept without question you may feel is provocative. A lot depends on personal opinions.

As more and more dance steps are being added to cheers each year, this is a problem that continues to grow. Each state has its own laws defining what is acceptable and what is not. The problem with these laws is that they do not make it clear how much is too much. When does a dance step become a sexual move?

Many believe that today's generation of cheerleader shakes way too much, to the point they call it dirty dancing. Many students disagree; they feel their rights are being violated by not being allowed to dance however they want.

Conservative dance with no provocative moves seems to be what each school is trying to maintain, but it is still a growing problem. Coaches work hard to keep their team dances clean. It is a hard decision as to what is too much, where do we draw the line? Parents input on this problem will help the coaches set guidelines for their cheerleaders that everyone can agree on.

Parents have a right to be concerned about their child's dance moves. Especially if they have a young child performing a provocative dance move in front of an audience. Again, getting involved is very important. If you don't like what you see, become a part of it to help make changes.

There are many parents and teachers doing everything they can to keep cheerleading clean. Let the girls show off their talent and skills, not their bodies. The more people involved voicing their opinions, the more can be done.

Many competitions have very strict guidelines concerning these issues. Uniforms that are too skimpy and many styles of dancing have been banned from competitions. If a squad breaks the rules by adding moves that are considered provocative according to their rules, the squad will be disqualified.

If a team arrives in a uniform that is against the rules of the competition, they will not be allowed to compete. Having these guidelines in place does help keep dance routines in cheerleading at an acceptable level. It also helps to relieve a lot of the concerns parents have on these issues.

Living On A Tight Budget

Money is always a parent's concern, how much is this going to cost? This is especially true if you are dealing with a tight budget. You may find buying the items needed for cheerleading very expensive. Even though it can be rather costly there are several ways of finding what you need. You don't necessarily have to buy everything brand new.

The uniform is the most expensive and is normally ordered through the school. Since this has to be exactly the same for everyone on the team your choices are more limited, but you can still find ways to cut the cost. There may be a relative or a friend that has outgrown their uniform and would like to sell it for half price.

Many schools offer an exchange system. If the school your child attends does not offer any programs of this nature you can help to get one started. Make a suggestion at the next PTA meeting. Or if you prefer you can talk it over with the coach to see how they feel about it. Discuss this issue with other parents, there are many others that would also like to save as much as possible. Parents whose child has outgrown their uniform would be happy to sell it for half price.

If you are looking for accessories you can shop around online. This is a terrific place to find companies that sell most anything for cheerleading you could think of. There are also sites like E-bay that sell many of these items at a very reasonable price.

Summary

Ultimately, any way you look at it, the best way for parents to deal with their concerns is by becoming involved. This way you have the opportunity to see and know what is going on. You have a chance to communicate with coaches and faculty members. Voice your opinion and be a part of the decisions being made.

JOINING A LOCAL CHEERLEADING SQUAD

A cheerleading squad is more than a group of people performing cheers together. You become teammates and learn to depend on each other. You work together to meet a common goal. You become friends and help each other, especially in difficult situations.

Most schools offer their students the opportunity to join a cheerleading squad. In the event that your school is small and does not offer this you can check into other options. There may be a cheerleading club in your area that you could join. Check with your local YMCA and other local organizations to see what they have available.

It doesn't matter if you want to tryout for a local cheerleading squad or one your school offers, the basic information needed is the same. Your next step would be gathering all the information available concerning the tryouts of the squad you are interested in.

You will need information like, when are the next tryouts? What expectations do they have for newcomers? Do they require you to perform certain moves at the tryout? If so, find out what they are so you can be practicing them in advance. The more information you acquire the better prepared you will be for the tryout.

Succeeding At Tryouts

Tryouts can be intimidating and make you feel uncomfortable. It may be the hardest step to complete because of the feelings you are experiencing. Even though it may be hard to control how you feel, you need to find a way to do so (the bonus book The Power of Concentration will help you here, if you read and practice the lessons inside). If you do not feel comfortable, your performance will suffer and limit your abilities.

There are several things you can do that will help you be successful at tryouts. Knowing what the judges are looking for and expecting from you will help out significantly. This will give you the chance to prepare yourself. Judges are not just looking at how well you know a cheer, but for many other qualities you may possess as well.

Self Confidence

If you want to be successful at tryouts, the first thing you need is self-confidence. If this is what you want to do, then know that you can do it. You don't have room for any doubts. Things will go much easier and more smoothly if you have a positive attitude. Judges will be looking for this quality in all the participants at the tryouts.

If you feel that you have a problem in this area you should work on your confidence before going to a tryout. If the judges notice you lack this quality they may choose someone else over you. It may be someone with fewer skills than you have, but who possess more self-confidence.

To help you build your confidence, you should practice as much as possible. If you know the cheers you will be performing you will be more confident that you can do them. Having confidence will make you feel more at ease in front of the judges. When you feel more comfortable at tryouts, you can focus on other aspects just as important as the cheer you are doing.

The more you have practiced the better you will execute your moves. You won't have to worry about your style and form suffering because you are trying to remember the words to the cheer you are doing. Judges know that you can learn new moves and routines but you can't really be taught how to be confident. This is something that comes from within the person. If they notice you have self-confidence they will be impressed.

Be Prepared

Being prepared when you go to a cheerleading tryout is extremely important. You wouldn't want to apply for any other positions and not be ready. If you don't know what is going on and what is expected from you, then it will be hard to make a good impression. You will appear to be a little lost and out of place. This will then make you feel uncomfortable and unable to fully concentrate.

First you need to gather all the information about the tryouts that you can. Find out if they require you to dress a certain way or if they leave it up to you. If it is your choice then decide ahead of time what you will wear. Waiting until the last minute may cause a problem.

If you wear long pants and a baggy shirt you will make it difficult for the judges to see what you are capable of doing. A nicely fitting tee shirt with shorts would be acceptable. If you have long hair remember to put it up or back out of the way. It just looks neater and will not interfere with your performance by getting in your eyes.

Always warm up before you begin the tryout. This will help you to be more flexible and physically ready to perform. It will help you feel relaxed and more comfortable. Pay attention to how clearly and how loud you speak. No one can use a cheerleader that is shy or cannot be heard. On the other hand, nether do you want to scream too loudly for the environment you are performing in.

Eye Contact

Always make eye contact with the judges. This lets them know you are sure of yourself and of your abilities. This is another quality they will be looking for. Keep smiling even if you make a mistake. They will be more concerned with how well you recover from a mistake than the mistake itself. They will note if you get frustrated or upset when you make a mistake. This will make the difference between whether they feel you can or can not handle the pressure of cheerleading.

Your goal is to show the judges that you can keep smiling and continue with the cheer under pressure. Don't give up or become distracted and they will see in you many of the qualities needed to become a cheerleader.

Enthusiasm

Keep your enthusiasm up at all times, but at a level that does not look like you are trying too hard. Tryouts may feel uncomfortable because there is no team playing and you may feel a little silly. Don't let this bother you. If you can't do cheers in front of a small group, how will you be able to perform in front of a large audience when many are depending on you? Let the judges see how supportive you can be for your team, even in uncomfortable situations.

These are some of the qualities judges will be looking for at cheerleading tryouts. Showing them that you posses many of these qualities will help you to make the cheerleading team. Just relax have fun and the rest will come.

CHEERLEADING CAMP

Going to a cheerleading camp is a great way to learn new techniques and improve on what you already know. These camps are offered to cheerleaders during the summer months. By attending one of these camps you can become more prepared for the new season coming up. When school begins again you will be ready for anything.

Cheerleading camp is a place where you can work together as a team in a relaxed environment. This is a great way for coaches to evaluate the squad as a team and as individuals. It will give coaches an opportunity to teach you new skills and to help improve the ones you already possess. If you were having problem performing any moves in the past season this is an opportunity for you to receive extra help in this area.

This is a great place for the team to bond together. Here you can become better friends and learn how to help each other. The better a squad communicates and works together, the more you can improve the squads overall abilities. You won't have a better place to improve communications between team members and coaches.

Improving Skills Without Classes

Going to classes to be trained for cheerleading is probably the best and easiest way to learn but not everyone may have this option. If you are one of these people don't worry, there are other ways to obtain the skills you need. You can visit several sites online that provide information on cheerleading that can be downloaded for your convenience. You can communicate through e-mail or forums that are offered by these sites. This is a quick and easy way for you to ask questions or add input you may have.

If you enjoy reading there is a countless numbers of cheerleading books at the library you can check out. You can find books explaining cheers and how they are done. You can read about professional cheerleaders and how many of them started out.

PROBLEMS & FEARS

As a cheerleader there are a lot of problems and fears you may encounter. Keep in mind that you are not alone. There are things you can do to help overcome these fears. Here are some problems that cheerleaders have faced in the past and suggestions as to how to deal with them.

Being Accepted

There are some people that just naturally seem to get along with and be accepted by everyone. They are very fortunate because this is not true for everyone. For some people it is hard to be accepted by others. They just don't seem to quite fit in. If you are one of these people then you will probably be worried about the squad accepting you. You may be surprised to know that many people have these worries and have to put forth a little extra effort to be accepted.

When you tryout for cheerleading, the squad are looking for many qualities. How well you carry yourself for instance. They will note how prepared you are and how quickly you pick up when shown something new. You will be judged by your abilities, not by who you are. Worrying about not being accepted will make you nervous. Then you might start trying too hard to fit in and cause problems. Try to relax. Remember, if you made the team you've already been accepted by the squad.

Letting The Squad Down

Every cheerleader has had the fear of letting their squad members down. Who wouldn't think of it at some point? Afraid you might make a wrong move or slip and fall. Not only would you be embarrassed but your whole team would be.

Even though it is natural to worry about things like this, keep in mind the squad is like your family. They are friends. They are your team mates and they will be behind you if you make a mistake. After all, they most certainly know how you feel. If you are not afraid of letting the squad down, the chances are you won't. If you do make a mistake, it's not the end of the world. Smile and keep on cheering, your teammates will be behind you.

Nerves

There is a time in every cheerleader's life when they are nervous and concerned about whether they will be able to perform. Everyone has doubts from time to time. Tryouts can always make you feel this way because you don't know what to expect. Competitions are another place where cheerleaders may find those nerves creeping in. Who will be the one you compete against? How good are they? You may even become so nervous you feel like backing out.

How do you deal with your nerves? Performing in front of so many people can be difficult. Having self-confidence will help but may not be enough when you look out and see a large audience waiting to watch you perform. This is when you just need a few minutes to be alone and relax. You know you have practiced long and hard for this opportunity. Now that it's here don't let it pass. Everyone is supporting you. All they expect or ask is for you to do your best. If you don't win, at least you tried and everyone will be proud of you for that.

Since nerves are mostly from mentally psyching yourself out, you can often ease the fears by just relaxing. However, there are other things that can help you as well. For one, be sure you practice and you know the routine well. This way you feel more confident in your abilities. You also need to be sure you get a good night's rest the night before. Lack of sleep will make you tired and your reflexes slower as well. You want to eat a well balanced diet and be well rested so that your body and mind are prepared. This will help ease your nerves.

If you don't want to eat right before the event, you might try a nice healthy snack like some fresh fruit. You need something to give you energy and stamina. Eating something, even something small will help you have the energy that you need and will help your brain as well. Your diet and health play a big role in your nerves and how you can deal with feeling nervous.

Jealousy And Lack Of Trust

Jealousy is a real issue and may be hard to deal with. When a person has held a position for a while and someone new comes along that can do that position better, this may cause some jealousy. Or maybe you tried out for a position and it was given to another person, this may make you a little jealous of them. Maybe you were the one who got a position over someone else and they are jealous of you. Either way there is no room for jealousy on any team, much less a cheerleading squad. If there is jealousy on your squad then you won't have trust.

Without trust you will not be able to perform as a team and work together. Trust is one of the most important aspects of cheerleading. It is what can make a team or destroy it. Each team member needs to know they can trust and rely on everyone on their squad.

Suppose you are a flyer and you are not sure if the base will hold you up, or let you fall. Not a very good situation is it? Suppose you don't trust the person that is supposed to catch you if you slip. You will be so busy thinking about it you won't be concentrating on what you are doing. Your performance will definitely be hurt and the whole team will suffer.

If there is jealousy and lack of trust on your cheerleading squad it needs to be dealt with. Since approaching the person would be hard to do and may cause more problems, you should take your concerns to the coach. Explain the situation and your concerns. You can go to the coach if someone is jealous of you or if you are the one feeling jealous. Either way, they will be able to provide you with a way to work things out. Sometimes just being able to sit down and talk about how you feel will solve the problem.

Talking To Your Coach

Communication is essential in cheerleading, especially between a coach and his or her team. A coach has to be able to teach and train the squad a lot of difficult moves. If there is a problem with communication this would be harder to do. Someone could get injured due to lack of communication. Your team would not be able to advance as quickly or easily as they should.

Not only is it important for a coach to communicate with their team, but the team needs to be able to talk to the coach as well. This is true even when it comes to private issues. One of the keys to having a successful team is having great communication. If a cheerleader has a personal problem that may interfere with their performance, they need to be able to discuses this with their coach. It may be something that can be worked out to everyone's advantage. If the communication is not there, a problem that could have been taken care of may turn into a problem for the whole team.

A cheerleading coach needs to let the squad know that they can come to them for help in any situation. It could make a big difference in how well the team does. As a cheerleader you should talk to your coach when there is a problem. Asking someone for help can really make a difference.

EXERCISE & DIET

A big part of becoming a cheerleader is being physically fit. This requires having an exercise program and balanced diet in place. It is important to be healthy for many reasons; the main one of course is so you will feel the best you can. Being healthy also helps to prevent injuries and gives you the energy you need to perform cheers.

Exercise Program

To be a successful cheerleader you need a good exercise program in place. There are three main issues to address when considering this exercise program, they are:

- Strength

- Flexibility

- Stamina

Without these qualities you will not be able to meet the demands that will be put on your body when you become a cheerleader. You need to make sure you have strength training included in your program. This is the quality that will help you perform many of the required cheers and stunts your squad will be doing.

Regardless of what position you hope to hold, you have to have strength to be able to handle it. If you are a flyer you need strength to climb and pull your own body weight. If you hold a base position you have to have enough strength to hold up other members of the squad. Suppose you hold a spotters position and a team member slipped and fell? Without strength training you wouldn't have a chance catching them.

Flexibility is just as important and will help you in many ways. Have you ever wondered how some cheerleaders can do moves like kicking, jumps and splits with so much ease? It is because they are very flexible. Their muscles are trained to perform these moves and can do them naturally.

Being flexible will also help to prevent injuries. The looser your muscles are, the more they stretch. Performing stretch exercises will help you to become more flexible. When you do stretch exercises make sure you never bounce, this can do more harm than anything. Instead you should just stretch and hold for ten or more seconds.

Stamina is a quality needed to help you last through a game. Without stamina you will become tired and give out sooner than you should. You not only have to be able to make it through a game but the whole season. This could be considered the most important physical condition needed to be a cheerleader.

One good way to build stamina is through an aerobic exercise routine. Aerobics increase your heart rate and metabolism which increases your energy levels. This is the best way to have the stamina you will need to be a great cheerleader.

If you are not used to an exercise routine you should start off slowly as not to cause any damage to your muscles, you want to build them not hurt them. Start out about three times a week for only ten to fifteen minutes a day, then as your body adjusts to this you can begin gradually increasing. Be sure and follow all safety precautions and guidelines when exercising.

Balanced Diet

Having a balanced diet is more important than you may realize. If your body does not get the proper nutrition it needs, you will not have the stamina or strength you need to be a cheerleader. You may do okay at first but with time you will begin to get worn down. Your body will not be receiving enough nutrition to keep you healthy. Your body needs a certain amount of carbohydrates, fats and proteins, to keep you healthy and energetic.

At first you may feel tired all the time and find that you have less interest in things you once loved. After a while you may become frustrated with yourself and others. Once this happens you may become negative and begin to have a bad attitude. Others will notice the change in your attitude and your performance. Without a proper diet you are setting yourself up to be let down.

With a balanced diet you will feel better and have more energy than you knew was possible. Having energy is not the only benefit from eating a well-balanced diet. It will also make a big difference in your mental ability. When your body is receiving the correct amount of vitamins you will be more alert and aware of your surroundings. Being alert will help you to learn cheers and routines much more easily. You may even be surprised at how much easier things seem to happen. It should even be simpler to maintain that grade level that is required by the school.

Make sure your diet includes the correct amount of nutrition needed for your body. You will feel much better and have a lot more energy to go around. Another plus to eating well is that it will be much easier to maintain your proper weight - something everyone is concerned with. Remember to never skip meals; this only hurts your body physically and mentally.

Ideal Weight For Different Positions

Maintaining an ideal weight will help you to get the position you seek. Each position has certain requirements that must be present to hold it. Your weight is one of these requirements. Your weight should be in proportion with your height to be considered ideal for any position.

To see why this is an issue, let's take an example. Imagine that you wanted to be a flyer, but you were twenty pounds overweight for your height. In this instance it would be hard for the base to lift you to the top of a pyramid. It would also be difficult for you to perform many of the other stunts involved in cheerleading.

When you maintain a weight that is right for your body it helps you to feel good. It helps to increase your energy levels making you more active. You may find it is easier to perform moves that you thought were too difficult in the past. Not only will you feel great but you will look great. Your weight does have a lot of influence on your overall general health. Find out what your ideal weight is and make an effort to hold that weight.

CHEERS, CHANTS & ROUTINES

Did you know there is a difference between routines, chants and cheers? Did you know that some cheerleaders participate at games while others compete at competitions? Some cheerleaders may even be present at both. This is something that is actually decided by the coaches you work with or the school you attend.

In a situation where you can participate for both, your coach should be the one you places you on a particular squad and decides which team you help support. The decision will be based on your qualifications and attitude. It will depend on your personal goals as well. For example, if you prefer to only cheer at games then you won't be forced to enter a competition. If competing is what you enjoy and you have a great attitude, most likely that's where you will end up. If you love both and have the time for both, coaches can always use a member of the team that can be flexible.

To be able to perform many of the requirements for cheerleading you need a wide variety of skills. You should be able to do gymnastics, tumbling and even dance moves. You need to be able to do splits or handsprings, and have excellent balance to build pyramids and perform other difficult stunts. Cheerleading is an activity that requires a lot of athletic abilities.

Cheers

Cheers are different from chants because they are usually performed during half times and other breaks during the game. They are longer and more specific than chants and include a variety of different moves. Cheerleaders use their imaginations to create cheers and stunts that are unique to their squad.

Cheers include a lot of different moves, everything from gymnastics to pyramids. Cheerleaders use jumps and dance in their cheers to make them more exciting. This is the opportunity that cheerleaders have to be creative. Many times the name of the school is used in cheers.

Chants

Chants are usually done when something exciting happens during the game. The cheerleaders begin to chant to help get the crowd motivated and enthused. The cheerleaders will gather together and yell a word or phase repeatedly while inviting the crowd to join them.

These chants are meant to both excite the crowd and encourage the players. They feel the adrenaline rushing through them while they hear the crowd going wild. Chants are usually performed throughout the duration of the game. Adding claps and stomping feet give power to chants and help encourage the audience to become involved.

Routines And Stunts

The more you learn about cheerleading the more you realize that sometimes cheers and chants are not quite enough to get the audience to respond. This is when routines and stunts are brought into play. Your team needs to practice to be good, because there is so much involved in these areas. The more you understand the basic required skills for routines, the better you can become. Below are some of these skills and a description of each.

Jumps

Jumps are a big part of cheerleading. They really get the attention of the audience because both feet leave the ground. Your body will assume a specific position while in the air then you return to the ground. Did you know there were several basic types of jump? Here is a list of the most important:

- Tuck

- Stag

- Toe touch

- Pike

- Doubles

- Hurdles

Did you know that there are three parts of a jump? Many people think all you do is jump up into the air, not realizing it's more complicated than that. The three parts to a jump are the approach, the jump and the landing. The way you approach the jump is very important, this is what will determine the direction of your jump and the initial lift off.

Lifting your arms during the actual jump is what helps you with your form and increases the height of your jump. It is very important to keep your body straight during this part of the jump. You want to make a smooth landing without stumbling and losing your balance. You should always make sure that your knees are slightly bent to help prevent injury. This also makes your jump look more professional.

By practicing these three aspects of the jump you can learn to jump higher and look more uniformed while doing so. You can prefect your take off and landings. Since everyone notices the jump so much, the higher and better you perform, the more excited the crowd becomes.

Another way of improving your jumps is to perform exercises. You can do toe touch exercises on a regular basis. For example, Toe Touch Drills. With Toe Touch Drills, you first want to stretch out properly and do some leg lifts. About three sets of leg lifts will be good. Then you want to do side high kicks. Do about 5 times with each leg while your hands are in a T formation. Now throw your toe touches. Try to hold to a count of eight each time, if possible. Do these in sets of 10. You will notice a huge improvement after performing these on a regular basis.

Splits

A split is when the cheerleader is in a position where their legs are sideways, one positioned in front of the other or spread apart in alignment. Anyone can do splits but some people are more flexible than others so you should start slowly. Never push to the point of feeling pain and never bounce; you want to use a smooth motion when doing a split to prevent injuries. The best way to improve a split is by doing stretch exercises that will help you to become more flexible.

Tumbling

Tumbling is simply a gymnastic skill that is integrated into a cheer or routine. It can be done by an individual or as a group. Using tumbling in your cheers is a great way to stir up the crowd.

Front Flips And Back Handsprings

Front flips are pretty self explanatory but still need to be done with grace and style. To perform a back handspring you need to start by positioning yourself just right, then you jump backwards on to your hands, next you push off with your hands landing back on your feet. Many cheer-leaders take gymnastics to help them be better at this.

Aerials

An aerial is a term used to describe a move like a walkover or cartwheel but without using your hands. The aerial is a difficult move and may not be used as often as many of the others.

Practice Sessions

To become a great cheerleader you have to be willing to practice. This is where and when you learn new cheers, dance and moves. It is also the only way to enhance the skills you already have. Practice does make perfect, the better you want to become the more you will need to practice.

Your cheerleading squad will meet several times a week for scheduled practices. It is very important that you make all of these meetings. You will go over routines you will be performing at the games and perfecting them as a team. This is the time you can receive help with any moves you may be having difficulty with.

Outside of team practices you can set aside certain times each week that you can practice on your own. You may find practicing in front of a mirror a big help, especially in perfecting your form. This gives you the opportunity to see the position of your body when you are doing a cheer. It will also allow you to see if you are smiling while performing your moves or if you are making other facial expressions.

Show how much you care about cheerleading by appearing at all the practice sessions prepared to learn. Be properly dressed and enthusiastic about having the opportunity to advance your skills. This will say a lot about your attitude towards cheerleading and help you to be successful.

GETTING THE POSITION YOU WANT

You have done everything needed and are ready to tryout for cheerleading; now you need to choose what position you would like to have. You have to be prepared to work hard to actually get the position you want. If you are not qualified for what you want you may be given a different spot.

To be qualified for the spot you want you need to know something about that position. Each position that a cheerleader holds has certain qualities needed especially for it. Here are the positions including a description of each.

Flyer

This is a popular position in cheerleading that many work very hard to obtain. The flyer is the person that is thrown through the air and then caught by other team members. This position can be known by different names such as a floater or mounted. This is because the flyer is also the one to climb to the top of pyramids and definitely receives a lot of attention.

The flyer requires the strength to be able to lift up their weight with ease. You have to climb other members of your team to perform many of the stunts. It is important that you can maintain balance throughout the entire stunt to make it as easy as possible. It would be difficult to hold you up if you are struggling for balance.

This position also requires the person to have a lot of trust and confidence in the other members of the team. You have to be confident that they will catch you or you will be too worried to concentrate on what you are doing. If you don't believe they will be there for you then you will not be able to hold this spot.

Spotter

The job of the spotter is to help the flyer mount and dismount from stunts being performed. The spotter helps support and balance the flyer. It is also their responsibility to help prevent an accident from occurring that may cause injury to the flyer. This is an enormous responsibility and takes a person that can think and react quickly if a situation arises.

The spotter should stay in eye contact with the flyer constantly during the entire stunt. This person may or may not be a part of the actual stunt. To be a spotter you have to have the strength to catch a flyer if they slip and fall during a stunt. You have to be ready to put their safety before your own.

Base

The base is what makes up the main part of the stunt that is being performed, the footing of a pyramid for example. This person has to be strong enough to help hold up their teammates and - like the spotter - help the flyer if the need arises. This is a difficult position to hold and requires a lot of confidence and strength. Everyone in the base position must have precise timing with each other to have control over the stunt being performed.

Hard work and determination will help you to receive the position you want to hold. If you don't qualify for the position you want when you first begin cheerleading, this is a goal you can work towards.

Whatever position you hold, it is important to be able to learn or memorize cheers. Of course the best way to do this is by practicing a lot, both with the team and on your own. If you have spent a lot of time practicing and are still having problems then here is a suggestion that may help. You can try learning the words to the cheer first. Other team members may have found neat little ways to help them remember cheers that they will share with you.

Once you know the words then you can associate the words with a specific hand motion or movement to help you remember the move. Once you know the cheer when you say a certain word you should begin to automatically make the right moves.

How To Improve Your Moves

Coordination is imperative in cheerleading. You have to be coordinated to be able to carry out many of the cheers and especially for any stunts your squad performs. A big part of being a great cheerleader is being able to execute moves. The better your moves are the better cheerleader you are. The best way to accomplish this is by knowing how to do the moves correctly and then improving on them.

First you should remember that it takes a lot of flexibility to perform some of these moves. It is important that you be in good physical condition when learning and performing the motions. One way to be sure you are in shape is by having a stretching routine in place. This will warm up your muscles and help you to better perform.

Stretching will also help with any stiffness you may feel after performing moves. Always take the time to stretch and prepare your muscles before practicing and before performing your routines. This will help you do them better and help prevent injuries.

There are several basic positional moves used in cheerleading that need to be learned. Once you learn how to do them correctly you can begin improving the way you execute them.

The main ones used are:

- Ready position
- Lunge
- High V
- Low V
- T
- Broken T
- Touch down
- Low touchdown
- Daggers

Remember that it is essential to learn how to do each movement correctly. This is the only way that the move can be perfected. Listen carefully to instructions and don't hesitate to ask questions if you are unsure.

Moves Expressed Through Body Movement

Another way that cheerleaders have to express themselves is through body movement. Cheerleading is a visual activity and needs added movements of arms and legs to grasp the audience attention. The way your arms are positioned along with the use of pom-poms can add enthusiasm to chants and cheers.

There are only a few basic moves you need to learn for your arms. When using them you must be sure that you do them with the precise movement required. That is to say, you need the exact timing combined with distinct motions. Arm movement is one of the first things to catch the audience attention. You take the basic moves and add different positions to create different routines and cheers. Using a partner can help improve your skills and create more variety in your routines.

Once you learn the basic arm movements you want to execute them as best as possible. A few tips that will help you to improve your moves are:

- Make a sharp motion when you perform your moves.

- Keep your hand straight and thumbs on the outside of hand.

- Keep your arm in a position where you can see it out of the corner of your eye.

- Stay relaxed.

- Practice in front of a mirror to see what your form looks like.

By learning and using these techniques you will be able to improve your skills and become a more qualified cheerleader. It will help you get the position you want by knowing what is required of that position and how to execute the moves correctly.

Dance

When dance is used in routines you are adding a smooth rhythmic movement to your style. Using a combination of dance and basic precision moves is a great way to improve your routines and make them more unique and interesting.

Dance movements added to arm movements can create unique and interesting cheers. Some schools have completely separate teams that are known as dance squads. By adding a dance routine to your cheers you spice things up a little, and create more excitement.

One important thing to remember when you want to improve your skills is to maintain a good exercise plan that includes strength training along with stretches for flexibility. Always eat a well-balanced diet. Next learn the correct way to perform the moves needed, and then practice until you have perfected each move.

COLLEGE CHEERLEADING

College cheerleading is more advanced than high school; you will be expected to be more attentive and prepared than you have ever been before. Even if you were a cheerleader in high school things will be different in college. They will have higher expectations and stricter rules.

Before trying out for college cheerleading, one of the first steps you should take would be to find out just what is expected of you. There may be other activities that the college would like for you to be a part of if you become a cheerleader. Your grade point average may be higher than was required of you before. The time that you need to put into cheerleading may be more than you first expected.

In college you may be entered into a lot more competitions. You will hear the words all-star teams mentioned often. The reason for this is because all-star cheerleading is the same as competitive cheerleading. It is simply teams that compete on regular bases. To be a part of an all-star team you will need to devote most of your time to cheerleading.

There will be a lot of practice sessions that you must be present for. Missing practices or games will not be acceptable. If you are to take part in a competition you must always show up and be prepared to do your best.

Once you reach college cheerleading you will notice that there is much more involved in the cheers and routines that you perform. You will still be doing many of the basic cheers plus more gymnastics, but most likely more dances will be added to these routines.

You will be learning how to do many stunts that are more difficult than you are used to. Since you will be competing more and at higher levels more will be expected of you. As with high school, there are things you can do to help you be successful when you first tryout for a cheerleading squad.

Personal Appearance

When you first sign up for tryouts you will be making your first impression. How you look at this time will say a lot about your personality. Coaches and other cheerleaders will notice how you carry and express yourself. They will be able to tell if you feel confident or if you seem unsure of what you can to do.

Once you arrive at the tryout before you even begin showing your talent the judges will be forming an opinion of you. They will be looking at your personal appearance, things like do you have good posture standing up straight when you walk, or do you slouch. They will notice if you hold your head high and proud or if you look scared and nervous feeling out of place.

Judges will note if you did your homework to find out the general rules for the tryout, this is important to let them know you are serious about becoming a cheerleader. Putting forth that extra effort can make a big difference in how the tryouts go for you. Things that may not seem important to you may be a big issue with the squad you are trying out for. If you show up for tryouts prepared and already following the rules this will make a great impression.

Let's take makeup for example, is wearing makeup allowed? Many cheerleading teams will allow you to wear light makeup while others will allow none. If you show up for tryouts wearing heavy makeup they may get the impression you are not really serious about making the team.

What rules do they have concerning your hair? Should it be pulled back or put up on your head? It would be a bad sign if you are the only one trying out with your hair flying in your face. This is especially true if you miss a few steps because you had to stop and move your hair out of your eyes. Not a good first impression.

What you wear is very important, so be sure and find out the dress code before trying out for a squad. You don't want to show up in an outfit that ends up making you feel embarrassed or out of place. Unless the rules specify exactly what to wear, a pair of shorts and tee shirt should be fine. Usually wearing basic colors like black and gray are the best. Always prepare your clothes ahead of time making sure they are freshly washed and pressed before taking them to the tryout.

Even the way you sit while waiting to show what you can do gives the judges information about you. If you sit up straight with good posture, you will look self-confidant and ready for anything. But if you sit bent over fidgeting with something you will appear to have low self-esteem and to be worried about the tryouts.

Attitude

Always have an "I can" attitude, never let anyone see you doubting yourself. If you don't think you can do it then others will have doubts about you too. If you give the attitude that you know you can accomplish your goals others will believe in you also. Try to perform with as much grace and style as possible. If you appear to be stiff and unsure of what you want to do next, you show signs of lack of confidence.

Just like in high school, judges will look at how well you respond to a mistake you made. They will note if you become upset, or completely distracted and off track. The way you should handle a mistake is to jump right back in there and continue like nothing happened. The quicker and smoother you respond to something that went wrong will make a huge difference in how you are rated as a cheerleader.

Let's face it, sometimes mistakes do happen but it's how you deal with them that is so important. You can be embarrassed or be nervous when your tryout is over, but while you are performing don't let it show. Judges are looking for people that can keep it together under any circumstances. They want to see you move with ease and grace even during embarrassing situations.

Judges are looking for people who can get along well with others. Cheerleaders have to work together as a team. They provide each other with strength to learn new things and push to be the best. Always treat everyone with respect and courtesy.

Skills

How much skill you actually have will of course be a big part of what the judges are looking for. They will judge you on how well you are performing your moves. They will watch you go through the motions of a routine or cheer from the beginning to the end noting if the moves seem to come naturally for you, or if you are struggling.

They will be looking at your style, are your arms straight and hands in the correct position? They will notice how well you can perform jumps and how much gymnastic work you include in your routine.

They will judge you on how well your dance moves are executed. Do you have rhythm gliding into each move, or do you seem to have difficultly performing dance moves. Everything that you do is important in determining if you make the squad or not. Practice and be prepared before signing up for cheerleading tryouts and everything will go smoothly for you.

Experience

It would be a good idea to provide a background history of your experience when you tryout for college cheerleading. This history will be taken into consideration. It will give the judges something to look at, and they will base their expectations to your previous experience.

If you do not have any prior experience this doesn't mean you will not be selected. If you show that you have the ability and attitude it takes to be a cheerleader, then you will be given a chance. It may be a littler harder for you at first and you may need to put forth an extra effort, but if cheerleading is what you really want to do, it will be worth it.

Physical Condition

If you are not in great physical condition you may find yourself in a lot of trouble. You may not be able to perform the moves necessary to do what is expected of you. Just like when you were in high school this is a very important aspect of cheerleading. You have to be in the best condition possible to withstand the vigorous routines that are performed.

You should have an exercise program already in place but if you do not, you must start one a few months before you sign up for a cheerleading tryout. If you are not in good physical condition before tryouts, you may be setting yourself up for a big let down.

You will be performing in many competitions with competitors that have been training for years. If you expect to do well, you have to be prepared both in body and mind. Strength training is essential in keeping your muscles strong enough to carry your weight through all the stunts you will perform. It doesn't make any difference what position you hold, for example if you are a flyer you still need strength to climb a pyramid or push off a jump. The more strength you have the better you can perform in any area.

Stamina is something you need, to be able to endure the long practice sessions you will be taking part in. You need stamina to be able to last through a game. Without it you could never make it though a whole season. Aerobic exercises will help build up your stamina. You will feel energetic and ready for anything when you have this type of energy.

Flexible is imperative for cheerleaders. You can not do many of the required moves if you are not flexible. The more flexible your muscles are the less chance you will pull or strain a muscle. You want the audience to see you perform your moves with ease, not straining to make a kick or jump. The more physically fit you are the easier you will be able to do the stunts and the less likely you will be to sustain an injury.

A good exercise program that includes strength training and stretches for flexibility will also help to improve your balance. Any position you hold will require you to have good balance. You could not perform stunts like the cupie or elevator where you are being held in the air with just the hands of a base person, without balance. It would be impossible for them to hold you up if you were not straight using smooth movements.

Your diet is just as important as a good exercise program. Your body needs proper nutrition to build strong bones and muscles. Eating a well-balanced diet will ensure your body is getting the vitamins it needs to be healthy. It will give you more energy and help increase your stamina. Make sure you always eat healthy meals and avoid diets that can be harmful to your body.

PREPARING FOR COMPETITIONS

Having a competitive edge is the way to win a competition. You will need to prepare as an individual and as a team to accomplish this. Outside of having skills there are three other areas that should be addressed. Being prepared in all these areas will help your team in any competition. They are:

- Physical

- Social

- Mental

Your overall physical condition and the condition of the squad play an important role in competitions. Are you and your teammates the correct weight for your height? Do all of you participate in an exercise program that includes strength training and stretches for flexibility? Does the whole squad eat balanced meals with the correct amount of vitamins and nutrition? If not everyone is ready and prepared for the competition it will affect the performance of the whole team.

Your social skills play a very important part in how well you do in competitions. Does everyone in your squad get along with others? What type of attitude do you and your teammates have towards other cheerleading squads? Does your team always treat others respectfully? You can be the best performing team in the competition, and yet lose due to your poor social skills.

Being mentally prepared is just as important as being physically prepared. You and your squad will be performing under pressure in front of large audiences, competing against highly qualified competitors. You will need to make quick split second decisions and be prepared for anything.

If you are not mentally prepared for a competition, you may not be able to handle it. It would not go over with the judges very well if you looked out at the audience and froze because you were not expecting such a big crowd. It would be equally as bad to forget what your next move should be due to mental fatigue. If you are not prepared for what a competition involves, you may become overwhelmed and confused.

Competitors

Whether you are trying out for a cheerleading team or participating in a competition, you will be faced with competitors with equal or better skills. Don't be intimidated by this. Instead let this be an inspiration for you to put forth more effort. You can accomplish whatever you set out to do as long as you have the desire to make it happen.

There will always be competitors that are better, but this just gives you something to work towards. Having the proper training and conditioning will improve your skills helping you to become one of the best cheerleaders of today. Never give up just because you went up against someone a little better, instead train more and improve. Next time you meet them, you can be the most skilled.

PROFESSIONAL CHEERLEADING

Many girls - and boys - dream of becoming a professional cheerleader. This may have been their goal since they were a small child. Maybe you became a cheerleader when you were in high school and realized that it is something you truly love. In this case, becoming a professional cheerleader would be something you could work towards.

This is obviously a goal that will take a lot of hard work. You need to practice many hours improving your talent and skills. Although being pretty may help it is just not enough to make it professionally. The stiff competition that cheerleaders face today can be quite challenging. You have to possess good looks plus many other qualities.

The better you take care of yourself the more advantages you will have. You need to be able to present yourself well and show you are intelligent as well as athletic. Although having a nice body will get attention, your skills are what actually get you the results.

Professional cheerleading was born when the Dallas Cowboy cheerleaders were brought into existence. This happened in the 1972-73 NFL football season. It all came about because of a man who had an idea he wouldn't let go of. His name was Tex Schramm and he was the Dallas Cowboys general manager.

He knew there had to be a way to bring more excitement to their football games. Eventually he came up with the idea that adding more glamour to the sidelines could be what was needed. At first he tried to hire professional models to stand at the sidelines but this didn't work out very well.

After careful consideration he decided to have special cheerleaders along the sidelines. He wanted to create a new type of cheerleader, ones that could hold a crowd's attention and add more entertainment to the sidelines. He wanted more than the normal chants and cheers.

Meanwhile, Dee Brock was managing a squad of cheerleaders located in the Dallas Ft Worth Metroxplex area. Mr. Schramm took an idea to Mrs. Brock to see what she thought of it. This is when the decision was made to add dance to cheerleading, creating a new type of cheerleader. Together they recruited a lady named Texie Waterman. Mrs. Waterman just happened to be one of the top dancers in America; the three set out to add style and choreography to cheerleading.

This quest began with sixty ladies auditioning for the positions and ended with seven. Once these seven were chosen they spent the summer in training with Mrs. Waterman as their teacher. Dance was added to the cheers and a new way of cheerleading was born. After this summer of special training was over, the red white and blue uniforms were given to the girls and it was show time. As we all know, this was a huge success, and the turning point of cheerleading as we know it today.

Becoming A Professional Cheerleader

Becoming a professional cheerleader is quite a challenge. Many think that because they were a cheerleader in high school and college they automatically qualify as a professional. This obvious is not true. Only the most qualified even get the chance to tryout, so you know your competitors are some of the best.

As with any position you decide to go after, the more you know the better off you will be and the better chance you have of acquiring that position. Having a general knowledge in many areas will help you succeed.

General Knowledge

You have to show that you have a number of different skills and qualities to make it professionally. Good general knowledge is one such quality; having a good general knowledge can really pay off. For example, at some point you may be asked to give an interview. This would be a great opportunity for you, but if you don't have a clue about the topic being discussed, it could be devastating.

You also need to show that you can present yourself in a professional way. If you don't know the answer to a question someone may be asking, at least you should be able to respond in a professional manner. This is much better than being caught by surprise with nothing to say.

Sports Knowledge

You need a basic knowledge of the sport you are cheering for. In other words if you are cheering for a football team you need to understand the basic rules of the game. The same goes for basketball, soccer or any game you support. It would be beneficial for you to know the name of each position played, and the responsibility of that position.

If you don't understand how the game is played, how will you know when to cheer or start the audience in a chant? Suppose in an interview you were asked a question about a position on the team you are cheering for? You would need to be able to understand the question and supply an intelligent answer.

Having this type of knowledge will help you to feel more at ease and comfortable when cheering on the sidelines. When you feel comfortable you perform at your best. It will help with self-esteem because you will know you are prepared to face any challenges that cross your path.

Knowledge of Dance and Style

Having knowledge of many dance moves and being able to correctly perform these moves is a positive feature to have. The more moves you know and the smoother you present them, the better odds you have of winning a position.

You must know how to control your facial expressions while performing, always smiling. It would be very distracting if your expressions are uncontrolled while performing. If you were struggling some, everyone would know. If you are smiling contentiously no one would suspect you may be having problems.

You must put a lot of emphasis on your moves, your clap must be tight and clear, your arms must be fully extended, and your leg movements must be perfect. Jumps need to be high and body kept straight, dance steps must be smooth and graceful at all times

Even your voice plays a huge part in becoming a professional cheerleader. You must have a clear voice that can be heard and understood. You can not lead a crowd in chants and cheers if no one can hear or understand you. Putting everything together can be more difficult than you may realize.

Tryout Knowledge

Tryouts can be very intense and difficult, especially since you know only a few can be selected. If you know and understand the terms that are used by professional cheerleaders you can make an impression on the judges and everyone concerned. It shows that you have done your homework and are serious about becoming a professional cheerleader.

You should know the different positions your hands can be in while doing a cheer. Understanding what the different terms mean is imperative, if you were asked to do a candle stick but didn't know what it was, you might feel pretty silly. Along with knowing what the stunt is you need to know the number of people needed to perform it. Here are some examples of these.

Basket toss is a stunt that consists of three or more base people. Two of the bases interlock their hands and toss the flyer up into the air. While in the air the flyer can perform any jump they like.

Candle stick is a cheer move where your arms are stretched straight out in front of you with your fists facing each other.

Cupie is when a flyer has both feet in one hand of a base person while this persons arm is fully extended.

Elevator is when two separate base people each hold a foot of a flyer at shoulder level.

The more you know and understand the better chance you will have to becoming a professional cheerleader. Do your research and know what will be expected of you. There may be a certain style of dance that the team you are trying out for would prefer to see you perform. On the other hand there may be some that they will not allow. You want to make a good impression not a bad one by doing something they prohibit.

Fitness

On a professional level, cheers become more intense and stunts become more dangerous. The same basic rules still apply as the ones used in college and high school, but physical fitness becomes even more important. Be sure you have an exercise program in place that includes strength training, aerobic exercises, and stretches.

Having a balanced diet is imperative also, a lot of people are depending on you. You wouldn't want to pass out in the middle of a performance from lack of nutrition. You will need all the energy you can manage to obtain so always eat well-balanced nutritious meals.

Sacrifices

When you are trying out for a professional cheerleading job you may find that the money is not what you expected. Most professional cheerleaders start at minimum wage for the rehearsals and games they attend. You may find it necessary to hold another job to help you support yourself. Holding a job and being a professional cheerleader doesn't leave much time for anything else. When trying to become a professional cheerleader, you have no choice but sacrifice much of your personal life at the beginning.

You have to be very careful how you live your life, if you are seen in the wrong places or talking to the wrong people it would be devastating to your career. The media looks for anything they can make a headline with; you have to be careful what you allow them to know. Don't take any chances being in the wrong place at the wrong time. Avoid any gossip that comes your way to avoid being dragged down with it.

Any Regrets?

With all the effort that is put into being a professional cheerleader you have to ask, if you knew it would take so much effort would you do it all again? I know that after a minute of looking back at how far they have come, most professional cheerleaders say "absolutely, yes". For many it was fulfilling a lifelong dream.

Professional cheerleaders not only enjoy having a front row seat at all the games, but they also do a lot of charity work. They touch the hearts of many in a lot of different ways. Being a professional cheerleader is an exciting and rewarding career no one could regret.

Rules & Regulations

There are many important things you need to learn if you decide to become a cheerleader. For example, did you know that there are rules and regulations that you have to abide by? Did you know that different states have different rules concerning cheerleading?

The United States has laid the foundation for many of the rules and regulations that have been set in place for cheerleading practice and competitions. Other countries have either adopted these rules or used them as a guide to make their own. Today many countries have rules and regulations that are very similar. Over the years, countries have realized that if they use similar rules and guidelines, competitions go much more smoothly.

Rules and regulations are also different depending on what level you are participating on. Even though different states have different standards, I can still give you a basic guide as to what you will need to know. Remember this is just a guide and you should find out exactly what rules apply in your state and at your cheerleading level.

Basic State Game Rules For High School

The rules state that you have to wear suitable clothing for practices. This would be clothing like shorts, tee shirts, sweats etc... You cannot miss practices, and you must arrive on time. If you don't have a choice and must be late or miss a practice session, notify your coach in advance. If you do not follow this rule, you will receive an 'unexcused absent' for missing the practice session.

You have to be at all games, if you cannot you must notify the coach in advance or this will result in an 'unexcused absent'. Three unexcused absents usually will get you taken off the team.

No gum or jewellery is allowed at practices or games. If you want to be a part of the half time action you have to be at the game early. This is when you practice and stretch before the game. If you don't show up for this practice, you don't participate.

Cheerleaders in high school must wear their uniforms to school on the days pep rallies are given and games are scheduled. You need to be present before the pep rallies begin to practice and help make sure everything is in order.

Many high schools compete in cheerleading competitions. Here are the general rules for these.

The squad has to be signed up and entered into the competition prior to the time the competition is scheduled to begin.

Routines and cheers can only last for two and a half minutes.

You must enter onto the floor quickly and well-organized, then leave the same way as soon as you finish your routine.

No spring boards are allowed.

No free falling or swan dives allowed.

These rules are set in place for high school because cheerleaders are under the age of eighteen and are still considered as minors. In some cases they may not have a lot of experience and would be more apt to try something that was unsafe to gain points. Schools and competitions need to do all they can to ensure the safety of these children. Having strict guidelines in place is one way to accomplish this.

College Rules

Once you are out of high school you are usually considered an adult and the guidelines may vary some, but many of the same rules still apply.

Here are the important rules and regulations for college cheerleading.

You must always have a qualified coach or advisor present at all times, including practice.

All safety equipment used must be appropriate for the stunt being performed.

The coach must take in consideration the limits and ability of their squad and not push them past their limitations. This must be done as a team, if one person has more talent than the rest of the team they can't be pushed to keep up.

All cheerleaders must receive proper training in all areas before attempting a stunt or any move.

An exercise program must be in effect that includes strength training and stretches. A stretch routine for flexibility should proceed and follow all activities.

Never perform any stunt without the proper spotters.

All partner stunts must be approved before being attempted.

Competition rules do vary a little at each event, but the basic rules are the same. The goal is to keep all cheerleaders safe while competing. Here are listed the general safety rules.

Always be represented by a qualified coach who takes into consideration the qualifications of their team before placing them in a level.

Have a plan in place in the event an accident does occur.

Soft sole shoes must always be worn.

No jewellery of any kind unless it is for medical purposes.

No drops are permitted unless you land on hands and feet first to prevent injury.

No tumbling while holding props.

When props are used they must be degraded safely when finished.

Front, back and side drops are not allowed.

No spring boards or mini-trampolines allowed.

Spotters must be present at all time.

These are just a few of the rules that apply to competitions. There are many other dangerous stunts that are prohibited. Always get a complete list of the rules for any competition you intend to enter.

Becoming A Cheerleading Coach

If you have decided to become a coach for cheerleading, you have an exciting adventure ahead of you. It will carry an enormous amount of responsibility, but it will be worth it. Part of your job will be to motivate and encourage your cheerleading squad. This can be done both as a team and on an individual level.

If you see a cheerleader who needs just a little extra push to meet their abilities, this will be one of your jobs. You are here to push the team and get them motivated, but don't push too hard. After you have been with your team a little while you will know how hard to push. Always let them know you believe in them, this will help the cheerleaders to believe in themselves.

It would be a nice touch to post their accomplishments on a bulletin board. This will help to encourage your cheerleading squad. Never focus on the negative, this will make everyone depressed and the whole team suffers. It is important to make sure that while your team is working hard practicing and preparing for those games, you have fun as well. Everyone performs better when they are happy and relaxed.

You must have strict guidelines that everyone knows and follows. If you have just one that breaks the rules, it hurts the whole team. Keep the rules posted in a convenient place and carry a copy to all your games. It would be a good idea to give a copy to each member of the team. This way they will be able to look over it any time they want to.

If you are teaching in high school, sending an extra copy of the rules home for their parents is also a good idea. This way everyone involved knows exactly what the rules state. This will leave no room for confusion - no one can say they didn't know. Things will go much smother when everyone knows exactly what is expected of them to become and stay a part of the team.

You must be organized at all times, if not how do you expect your team to be? If you spend time fumbling and are not sure what should be happening next, your team will be confused as well. Some may even be roaming around not knowing what to do. You can keep a notebook with you to keep notes in, this puts everything at your fingertips.

When you first begin the season it is important for your team to know how you expect things to be done. For example, do you plan on letting your team participate in competitions? If so, cheerleaders and their parents need to know this in advance.

They will also need to know what time to set aside for practice, or any extra activities you want them to participate in. Some of these could include things such as a little community service to help build the team's image. Your team will follow your example so be sure and make it a good one.

Remember communication is imperative for your cheerleading team; you can't coach a team that does not understand you. They have to completely comprehend what you expect before they can attempt to learn. Always have patience with your team, being positive under all circumstances. You don't want to discourage your team by not having good communication with them.

Having communication on an individual level is also necessary. If your team knows they can talk to you on this level it may help avoid many problems before they occur. Let your team know that your door is always open.

Communication is not just important between you and your team, but with everyone. There are a lot of people associated with your cheerleading team. For example, if you are coaching a high school team, staying in touch with the parents will be beneficial.

You and your team need to stay in touch with other coaches, faculty members and the school board. This is true for anyone that affects your team. Cooperation with others will help you to be successful. Always be polite and courteous to everyone and you will pass this quality on to your cheerleading team. Never show any negativity, always be supportive even when there are a lot of improvements needed.

Coaching Tips

Here are some coaching tips that you should find very useful.

Remember to put the health and welfare of your students first and foremost above all else.

Promote safety rules encouraging your cheerleaders to be safe and follow all safety rules.

Remember your squad looks up to you and will follow your lead, always set a good example.

Never make the team feel like being the best at everything is all that matters. As long as they give it their best, that should be all you ask of them.

Pep talks do help and so does praising your team for a job well done.

Always act in a dignified manner during practices and at games. Treat opposing teams with respect even if they win.

Be there for your squad at all times ready to listen to their questions and concerns.

Always have a back-up plan, just in case.

Have A Game Plan

Coaches must have a team game plan for the whole season. This plan will include things like the teams you will be competing against, when the games will be played, and where they will take place. Schedules of all practices and meetings should be included. Have alternative dates scheduled in advance in the event something happens and a game gets cancelled.

In your game plan you should have a section where you assign specific duties to certain people. This way everyone always knows what they are supposed to do. There could be nothing worse or more embarrassing than to show up at a game and the whole team stands around wondering what to do. No one knows where to go or what they should do first. Here are some examples of what you may need to include in this section:

- Who calls the chants.

- Who is in charge of spirit items and props.

- Who handles the music.

- Who leads the cheers and routines.

- Explain how the line up will be handled throughout the game.

Another part of this section should include what steps you intend to follow in case someone unexpectedly does not show up for a game. Be sure and have a scheduled time for a warm up routine. Make sure everyone knows where and when this will take place. This is a great to time to add encouragement and support to your team just before they head for the sidelines.

It is always a nice touch for a couple of the cheerleaders to greet the visiting team. If you decide to do this, have a set schedule prepared for it. Pick out the cheerleaders that you want for this job and have them fully trained on how you would like this to be done.

They will need to know how to approach the visiting teams and what to say. Having this planned before hand will help avoid saying something the wrong way, possibly offending the opposing team.

As a coach you will find that you should always expect the best but be prepared for the worst. If something does happen at a game, call a time out. This will give you an opportunity to regroup and get your squad back on track.

Pep Rallies And Spirit Ideas For Coaches

It will be the coach's responsibility to come up with ideas for pep rallies. You need fun and original ideas and you want to make these events as exciting as possible. You may decide to have a special way to open and close the pep rallies. You can include your school mascot by letting him perform at the rallies.

You can add spark to your rallies with face painting or fancy dress. The use of props and signs can help to draw attention. Your goal is to get the audience involved as much as possible with songs and cheers. You want to show how proud you are of your school teams. You need to look for ways to get your school excited and ready for a game.

You can include a contest between classes or teachers at pep rallies. This is an opportunity to help bring unity to your school. Always be prepared for pep rallies by being organized and have all the details taken care of before you begin. At all times try to follow your schedule so things don't become confusing.

Finding The Equipment You Need

Uniforms used in cheerleading can be very expensive. As the coach, choosing uniforms is part of your responsibility. You need to take into consideration the expense when picking out uniforms for the team. Style is another big issue; you want to choose an outfit that will fit you team and their personalities, but which won't date quickly.

The correct shoes are needed to help prevent injuries. It is up to you to make sure your team understands the importance of wearing the right shoe and enforcing this rule.

Remember this is for their protection to help prevent ankle injuries.

Along with outfits you will need mats, megaphones, pom poms and many other accessories. Much of the equipment can be purchased online at discounted prices. Sometimes other schools and organizations have auctions or sales on their equipment. If you are working on a low budget this would be a great way to accumulate the equipment needed. You can also hold a fund raiser to help provide money for equipment.

Finding Competitions

It is part of the coaches' responsibility to find and enter their cheerleading squad in competitions. There are many different competitions held each year that are led by different companies. Some of these companies are:

- Universal Cheerleading Association

- American Cheer Power

- Cheerleaders of American

- National Cheerleading Association

These Are just a few of the companies that run competitions. You can visit sites online that will give you a complete list of competitions and where they are located.

How To Enter Competitions

Competitions are set up all through the year at many different levels and locations. As the coach it is your job to make the arrangements to enter them. There are a few important details to follow when entering your team.

First it is very important to make sure you enter your team in the correct competition. You need to make sure that you don't jump into a competition that is over your head. Putting your team up against teams that are well above their league could cause everyone to become discouraged.

If your school is a newcomer to competitions, you want to start with small local ones that have only a few competitors. This will help to get your team started and will build their confidence. Always look for the events that let you compete with other teams of equal level. In other words, don't go up against a team that has been competing for years when it's your first time.

Only choose to move up to new levels when the whole team has mastered the level you are now on. You can't move up just because a few may be ready. This wouldn't be fair to the ones that are not ready and can cause serious problems.

If you try to start out at the top you set yourself and your team up for a lot of disappointments. This can cause your team to become depressed and give up. They may have the ability to do great if started out on their own level.

Before entering your team in a competition, you want to do research on the organizing company. You need to make sure they have been around for awhile and are a legitimate business. You don't want someone who may end up cancelling events on your team.

Learn what is expected from your team before signing up for a competition. This way you know for sure it is something suited for them.

What To Expect From Competitions

Cheerleaders train all year to perform two and a half minutes in each competition they enter. It is a lot of preparation that goes into this short period of time. Cheerleaders will do a combination of gymnastics, cheers and stunts that are very difficult to perform, and will do them with grace and style.

When you are first sign up for a competition, teams are divided in two separate categories based on their age group and how difficult their routines are. They will compete against others who fall into the same category.

When you perform at a competition, all team members will be expected to have matching uniforms, and soft sole shoes. You will be expected to know - and follow - all the rules and regulations of the competition. Make sure your team is well informed.

Points You Will Be Judged On

When your team is performing there are several areas they will be judged on. Of course they will look at things like, did the whole routine go smoothly, or did you have difficulty in some areas? They will notice if each member of the team worked together well and if they were organized. They will look at did the climax of the stunt go as planed and how well your team exited the stunt.

It is important that when you present your cheers, you do so loud enough. The judges need you to be loud, but at the same time not sound like you are screaming out of control. Your voice needs to be crisp and clear so it will be easy to understand your words.

It is also very important to know how to make an entrance. Your team should enter the event in an organized fashion, not scattered about. After finishing the routine judges will also note how you exit the room. Everything you do is observed and taken into consideration.

The routine itself is judged on how authentic and original it was, and how well it was presented by the team. Your whole team will be judge on how professional each member performed throughout the entire routine. This is not the time for a member of the team to become concerned with personal issues. For example, make sure your hair is tightly secured back so you wont have to stop and put it back up during the routine. Be sure your shoe laces are secured and won't come untied during the performance; it would be very distracting to have to stop and tie your shoe, or fall because you didn't.

Summary

Cheerleading originated in America in the late nineteenth century and has been growing ever since. It has gained a lot of recognition and respect since its beginnings. It started with one man and has ended up with millions of people spread across the world.

Cheerleading requires many fascinating qualities. Being a cheerleader shows leadership abilities and a positive attitude. It is a great way to build self confidence. Cheerleaders work together as a team with no particular person standing out. The whole team works together to present the final spectacle.

Cheerleaders uses their cheers and chants combined with routines to reach out and grab the crowd's attention. They can take a boring game with little excitement and make it interesting and fun. They can add to the enthusiasm of a great game. Everyone expects cheerleaders to be on the sidelines of their favorite sport.

The use of gymnastics plays an important role in cheerleading. Combine this with song and dance and you have everyone's attention. At times, cheerleading has been considered a dangerous activity, even though compared to sports like football and basketball, far fewer injuries have been recorded. With the safety guidelines that are in place today cheerleading has been able to overcome these worries.

Every cheerleading squad has a signature cheer that is unique to their team. This is a tradition that will probably last as long as cheerleading itself will be with us. Most of the time it includes the name of the school or organization that the team is affiliated with.

All-star or competitive cheerleading can consist of a small or large group of men and women performing their best stunts and routines. They only have a few minutes to perform, but what they can accomplish in that time can be quite amazing. Cheerleading is an exciting and fascinating activity, sport, and for some - profession.

Printed in Great Britain
by Amazon